IN THE ZONE

FOOTBALL

TANIS BOOTH

Published by Weigl Publishers Inc.
350 5th Avenue, Suite 3304, PMB 6G
New York, NY 10118-0069

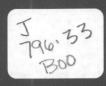

Website: www.weigl.com

Library of Congress Cataloging-in-Publication Data

Booth, Tanis.
 Football / Tanis Booth.
    p. cm. -- (In the Zone)
 Includes index.
 ISBN 978-1-60596-126-2 (hard cover : alk. paper) -- ISBN 978-1-60596-127-9 (soft cover : alk. paper)
 1. Football--Juvenile literature. I. Title.
 GV950.7.B66 2010
 796.332092--dc22
 [B]

                        2009005604

Printed in China
1 2 3 4 5 6 7 8 9 13 12 11 10 09

All of the Internet URLs given in the book were valid at the time of publication. However, due to the dynamic nature of the Internet, some addresses may have changed, or sites may have ceased to exist since publication. While the author and publisher regret any inconvenience this may cause readers, no responsibility for any such changes can be accepted by either the author or the publisher.

Every reasonable effort has been made to trace ownership and to obtain permission to reprint copyright material. The publishers would be pleased to have any errors or omissions brought to their attention so that they may be corrected in subsequent printings.

Weigl acknowledges Getty Images as its primary image supplier for this title.

Illustrations
Kenzie Browne: pages 9, 10 Left.

Heather C. Hudak Project Coordinator
Terry Paulhus Design
Kenzie Browne Layout

IN THE ZONE

CONTENTS

What is **Football?**

Football is a game of skill and physical strength.

Football probably began in England around 1820. A soccer player got bored with using only his feet to move the ball. The player picked up the ball and ran with it, changing the rules of soccer. This sport became known as rugby. It came to America in 1850.

In rugby, players can both kick and run with the ball. It was played at some East Coast colleges in the United States. Americans made some important changes. They used an egg-shaped ball instead of a round one and kept score differently. Americans renamed this game football. Football is now one of America's favorite sports to play and to watch on television.

In the 1800s, football looked very different from games that are played today.

Football is played by two teams of 11 players. The teams take turns being on offense and defense. When a team is on offense, its job is to score points. A player can score points by kicking the ball, passing the ball to a teammate farther up the field, or running with the ball. The defensive team's job is to stop the other team from scoring points and to keep the ball from moving forward.

A team has four chances to score a **touchdown** or to move the ball ahead enough to get another four chances. Each chance is called a **down**. If the offensive team does not move the ball far enough in four downs, it becomes the other team's turn to try to score points.

Sports History

Read about the history of the National Football League at www.nfl.com/history.

Football teams wear uniforms when they play. They also wear equipment under their uniforms. Football is a rough game, so it is called a **contact sport**. When a player has the ball, there is always an opponent whose job is to take it away. Football equipment is very important because it helps protect a player from injury.

A helmet and face guard protect the player's head and face. Each helmet has soft padding inside, which adds further protection. The helmet has a face guard to protect a player's eyes, nose, and jaw. A mouthpiece must also be worn to protect the player's mouth and teeth.

Players wear jerseys with their number on the back. They fit over padding to protect the players. Players wear separate pads for their ribs, arms, and often elbows. This saves their muscles and bones from injury after **tackles**.

Football players wear tight-fitting pants so the players are harder to hold on to. These pants fit over padding that protects the player's legs. Players wear thigh and knee padding when they are on the field.

Players wear shoes called **cleats**. They have spikes, or pieces of plastic, on the bottoms. This helps them grip the ground and not slip on the grass or **turf**.

The inside of a football is like a very strong balloon. This balloon is called a bladder and is covered with brown leather. White laces are on one side of the football. These laces help the player grip the ball. Gripping the ball is important when a player is trying to throw it a long way.

■ Some football players wear gloves. This helps them hold on to the ball. When it is raining, the ball can get slippery.

■ There is a goalpost at each end of a football field.

■ Footballs come in different sizes for different sized hands.

7

The Field

A football game takes place on a large, rectangular field. An American football field is 160 feet (48 meters) wide and 360 feet (110 m) long. Surrounding the rectangle are thick white lines to mark the boundary. The long part of the field is called the **side line**. The short part of the field is called the end line. At each end of the field are goalposts. Goalposts are in the **end zone**. The end zone is where a touchdown is scored.

The two teams switch from offense to defense throughout the game. **Possession** of the ball changes from team to team several times. The team with the most points at the end of four 15-minute quarters wins the game.

■ The Orange Bowl Stadium in Miami is an outdoor football field. It holds 74,000 people.

Sports Venues

To read more about football fields, turn to http://entertainment.howstuff works.com/football1.htm.

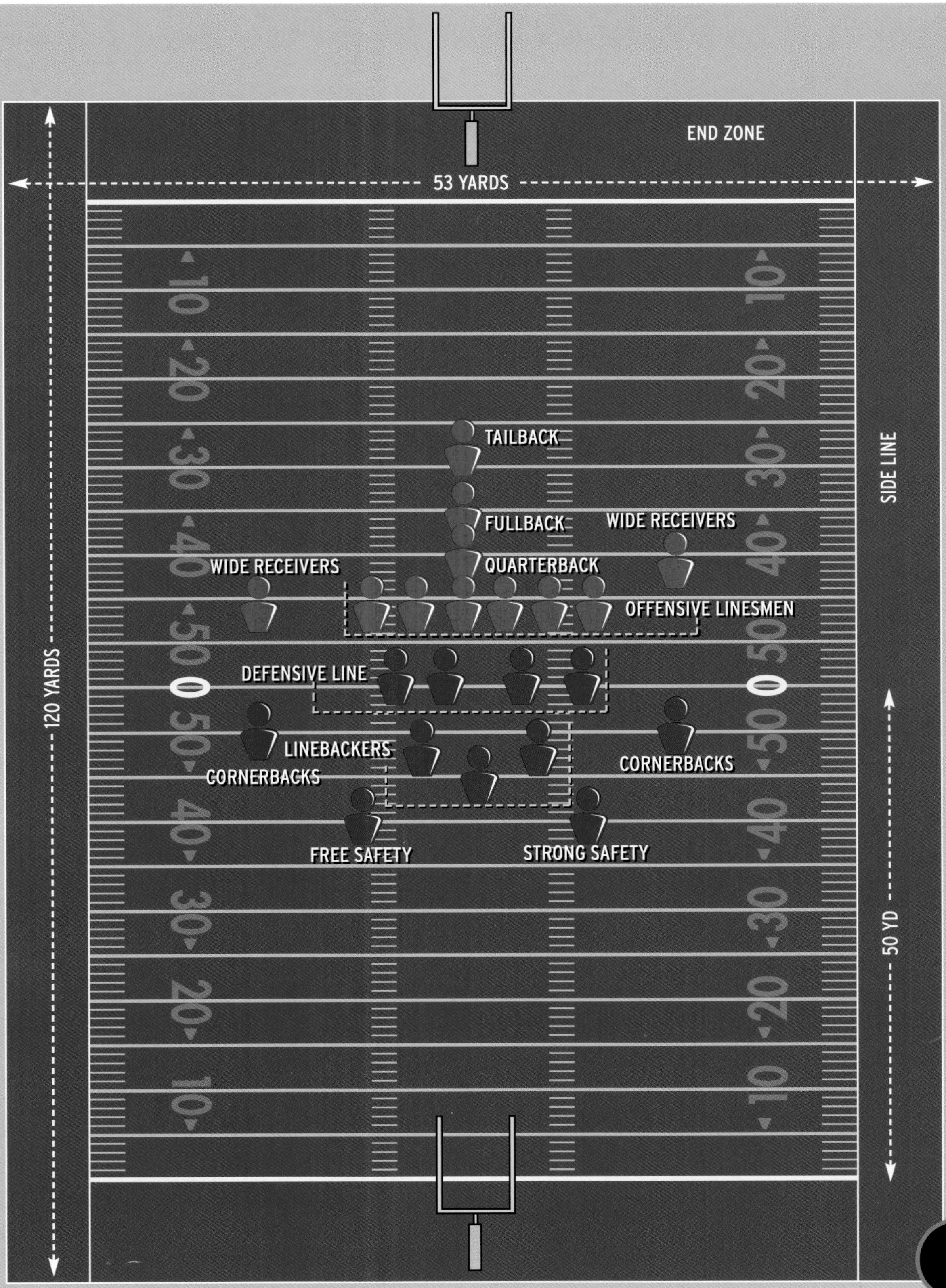

END ZONE

53 YARDS

10

20

30

40

10

20

30

40

50

50

SIDE LINE

120 YARDS

50 YD

TAILBACK

FULLBACK

WIDE RECEIVERS

WIDE RECEIVERS

QUARTERBACK

OFFENSIVE LINESMEN

DEFENSIVE LINE

LINEBACKERS

CORNERBACKS

CORNERBACKS

FREE SAFETY

STRONG SAFETY

40

30

20

10

The main goal in football is to score touchdowns. This is achieved when a player runs across the end zone while holding the ball. A player also scores a touchdown if he or she catches the ball in the end zone.

Each team gets four chances, or downs, to score a touchdown. A team must move the ball at least ten **yards** down the field in order to get another four downs. The other team tries to prevent any touchdowns. They tackle players and block the ball. Another way to prevent a touchdown is to catch a pass from the other team. This is called an **interception**. When a player intercepts a ball, his or her team switches from being on defense to offense.

Hand Signals

Referees use hand signals. These are a few examples.

Referee

HOLDING

TIME OUT

PASS INTERFERENCE

ILLEGAL MOTION

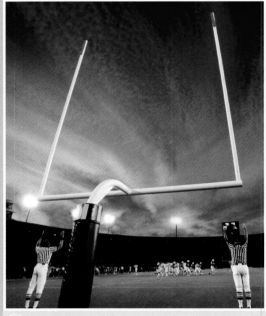

■ The officials wait in the end zone when the ball is kicked. They throw their arms up when a field goal is scored.

■ Referees sometimes take measurements of the ball's location on the field.

A team can also score points by kicking a field goal. After a touchdown, the team can try kicking the ball through the goalposts. The player who kicks the ball is called a place kicker or kicker. The ball must go between the two posts to score points.

A different number of points is given for different ways of scoring. A touchdown is worth six points, a field goal is given three points, and kicking the ball through the goalposts after a touchdown is worth one point.

■ The kicker only comes on the field when it is time to try to score a field goal.

■ The opposing team must try to stop the team with the ball from scoring a touchdown.

Sports Rules

For more on football rules, surf over to
www.getintoamericanfootball.com.

E ach team carries approximately 40 players. Only 11 players from each team are on the field at once. There are many different positions. Certain skills make players good at certain positions.

Some offensive players are small and fast. They are passed the ball, and they run down the field with it. These players are called receivers. Receivers have very strong leg muscles because they need to reach a top speed quickly and keep that speed for a short time.

■ Receivers move the ball toward the end zone. They keep the ball tucked close to their bodies. This prevents them from dropping it.

■ Each player has a certain position on the field. Players move after the referee blows the whistle.

The quarterback is the player who decides the plays for the rest of the team. The team gathers on the field in a tight circle before a play starts. This is called a **huddle**. It is the quarterback's job to call the plays during the huddle and to make sure all of his or her teammates understand the play.

Other players called linesmen take on defensive positions. They are usually bigger and stronger than offensive players. Linesmen block or tackle players from the other team. Each offensive and defensive position is broken down into more specific but similar positions.

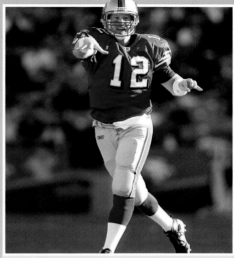

■ The quarterback is the player who usually passes the ball. The quarterback requires a great deal of skill and accuracy when throwing a football. He or she has to make the ball spin as it flies through the air. This is called a spiral.

■ Players can get hurt when they are tackled.

The Super Bowl

Children interested in learning to play football join community football teams. They can also play on junior and senior high school teams. From there, many try out for college or university teams. College players compete in the National College Athletic Association (NCAA).

College football is very similar to the National Football League (NFL) but has a few differences in scoring. Colleges also have wider goalposts. The college championship game is called the Orange Bowl. Young players who win the Orange Bowl can draw the attention of professional teams.

■ Many young athletes start out playing football in the school yard.

■ Winning college games is very important. It helps players catch the eye of professional scouts.

There are different football leagues for college and professional teams. At one point, there were both the American Football League (AFL) and the National Football League. Now, the NFL is the official league for professional football players in the United States.

■ Extra players watch the game from the side lines.

The first championship game in the National Football League took place in Chicago in 1932. In 1969, the championship game became known as the Super Bowl. The Super Bowl is now a famous sporting event that is watched by millions of people across America. The Super Bowl is held in February each year.

■ The competition in the Super Bowl is fierce. Players do all they can to win the game.

Football has had many heroes. They were often the inspiration for today's players.

Joe Namath

POSITION: Quarterback
TEAM: Los Angeles Rams
SIGNED TO THE NFL: 1965

CAREER FACTS:

- Joe played with the New York Jets until 1976. He played for the Los Angeles Rams the following year.
- Joe was the first player to pass more than 4,000 yards in one season.
- After retiring in 1977, Joe became a successful football broadcaster.
- Joe was named to the AFL All-Star team three times.
- Joe starred in Hollywood movies.

Walter Payton

POSITION: Running Back
TEAM: Chicago Bears
SIGNED TO THE NFL: 1975

CAREER FACTS:

- Walter held the record for rushing, or covering a great deal of the field by running and moving the ball forward.
- Walter played for the Bears for 12 seasons and scored 125 touchdowns.
- After his retirement, the Bears retired his number. No other player on that team would ever be able to wear #34 again.
- Walter was voted the NFL Player of the Century by football fans. He was made a member of the Pro Football Hall of Fame in 1993.

88

Lynn Swann

POSITION: Wide Receiver
TEAM: Pittsburgh Steelers
SIGNED TO THE NFL: 1974

CAREER FACTS:

- Lynn was the number one draft pick.
- In 1993, Lynn was named the Best Athlete of All-time.
- During Lynn's nine professional seasons, he played in four Super Bowls and was named the Most Valuable Player in the Super Bowl twice.
- Lynn holds the Super Bowl records for the most yards gained receiving, at 364, most receptions, with 16, and most touchdowns, with three.
- Since 1980, Lynn has been the national spokesperson for the Big Brothers and Big Sisters organizations.
- After retiring, Lynn became a football broadcaster.

19

Johnny Unitas

POSITION: Quarterback
TEAM: Baltimore Colts
SIGNED TO THE NFL: 1956

CAREER FACTS:

- Johnny led the Colts to championship titles in both 1958 and 1959.
- In 1979, Johnny became a member of the Pro Football Hall of Fame.
- Johnny was named the Player of the Year in three separate years.
- Johnny threw at least one touchdown pass in 47 straight games.

The stars of today have fans cheering in the stands every week.

Eli Manning

POSITION: Quarterback
TEAM: New York Giants
SIGNED TO THE NFL: 2004

CAREER FACTS:
- Eli was named MVP at Super Bowl XLII.
- In 2004, Eli was the number one draft pick in the first round.
- Eli was named NFC Offensive Player of the Month in November 2008.
- In December 2008, Eli was named to his first Pro Bowl selection.
- In 2007, he began raising money to fund The Eli Manning Children's Clinics.

Larry Fitzgerald

POSITION: Wide Receiver
TEAM: Arizona Cardinals
SIGNED TO THE NFL: 2004

CAREER FACTS:
- Larry was drafted third overall in the 2004 NFL Draft.
- Larry was named to his first Pro Bowl in 2005. He received MVP honors at the 2009 Pro Bowl.
- At the 2008 NFC Championship, Larry tied an NFL record with three touchdown receptions in one playoff game.
- He played in Super Bowl XLIII.

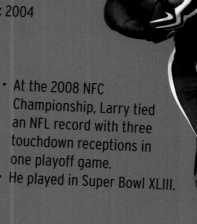

Tom Brady

POSITION: Quarterback
TEAM: New England Patriots
SIGNED TO THE NFL: 2000

CAREER FACTS:

- Tom is thought to be one of the best quarterbacks of all time.
- He has played in four Super Bowls and has won three of them.
- Tom has two Super Bowl MVP awards.
- He is the NFL record holder for having the most touchdown passes in a single season.
- Tom won his first 10 playoff games, setting an NFL record for the most consecutive wins in playoff games.

Willie Parker

POSITION: Halfback
TEAM: Pittsburgh Steelers
SIGNED TO THE NFL: 2004

CAREER FACTS:

- Willie's exceptional speed has earned him the nickname "Fast Willie."
- He won the award for the Longest Touchdown Run in Super Bowl history at 75 yards.
- In 2006, Willie was the Pittsburgh Steelers Team MVP.
- Willie has been clocked in at 4.23 seconds for a 40-yard dash.

Sports Heroes

To find out more about the NFL and its superstars, check out www.nfl.com/players.

19

Athletes need to drink plenty of water to replace what their bodies lose through sweat. When muscles are working hard, they produce heat in the body. In order to keep a cool temperature, the body releases heat through sweat.

Athletes also need a healthy diet. Doctors who work in sports medicine say that a healthy diet helps prevent injuries. If an athlete does get injured, a healthy diet encourages bones and muscles to heal faster.

■ It is important to drink water while playing sports

Eating a balanced meal allows athletes to exercise for longer periods of time without getting tired. This means that all athletes should eat meals and snacks from all the different food groups. Foods from different food groups, including fruits and vegetables, milk products, breads and cereals, and protein, have important **nutrients** needed for a healthy body.

■ Fruit is a good source of vitamins. It gives people quick bursts of energy.

Many athletes enjoy eating big meals the night before a game. Foods such as spaghetti, rice, breads, and vegetables are popular because bodies store them as energy in their muscles. Football players use this energy when they play. It helps them last until the end of the game. To stay healthy on the field, players also stretch and warm up their arms, legs, and back. This helps keep their muscles strong and injury-free.

■ While meat is important for protein, eating plenty of vegetables helps keep athletes strong and healthy.

■ Stretching during the pre-game warm-up helps to prevent injury.

Football Brain Teasers

Test your knowledge of this great sport by trying to answer these football brain teasers!

Q What does NFL stand for?

A NFL stands for National Football League.

Q What is the name of the college championship game?

A The college championship game is called the Orange Bowl.

Q When is the Super Bowl held?

A The Super Bowl is held in February each year.

Q How long is a football game?

A Each quarter is 15 minutes long, so a game is one hour long.

Q Why does a football have laces on it?

A A football has laces to help a player grip the ball when throwing it.

Q Who holds the NFL record for having the most touchdown passes in a single season?

A Tom Brady is the NFL record holder for having the most touchdown passes in a single season.

Glossary

cleats: special athletic shoes with small spikes or tips on the bottom; they help players stop or turn quickly

contact sport: a sport in which physical contact between players is allowed

down: one of four chances to move the ball 10 yards down a football field

end zone: the end of the field where a touchdown can be scored. The goalposts are in the end zone.

huddle: a small circle of players on the field; plays are discussed in huddles

interception: when a player catches a pass from the opposing team

nutrients: substances needed by the body and obtained from food

possession: control of the ball; being on the offensive

side line: the long part of the field marked by a thick white boundary

tackles: throws or drags down in order to stop advancement

touchdown: scoring by catching or running the ball into the end zone

turf: artificial grass or field made of human-made material

yards: measures of distance on a football field; a yard is equal to 3 feet (1 m)

Index